THE OPERATIC MUSE

An Exhibition of Works from
the Robert L. B. Tobin Collection
Honoring the 30th Anniversary Season of
the Santa Fe Opera

MUSEUM OF FINE ARTS, Museum of New Mexico,
Santa Fe, New Mexico, June 28–August 31, 1986

THE TOBIN WING, Marion Koogler McNay Art Museum,
San Antonio, Texas, September–December, 1986

Published through the courtesy of the Tobin Foundation, San Antonio, Texas
© Copyright 1986 Marion Koogler McNay Art Museum
ISBN 0-916677-07-9
Library of Congress Catalog Card No.: 86-42668
Printed in the United States of America

THE OPERATIC MUSE

For Donald Gramm

115. Jo Mielziner, *The Emperor Jones,* Design for the Décor, "The Throne Room", 1931.

THE OPERATIC MUSE

Musing about opera has numerous advantages weighed against certain drawbacks. At least it has been a source of diversion for centuries.

From a social historian's point of view, opera has the distinction of having been created at a certain time and certain place by a certain group. Rather like a Renaissance version of a Louis Auchincloss Study Club, the *camerati* did what Bárdi set out to do: to bring antique drama to contemporary life. The date was the last of the sixteenth century, the place was Florence and the young men were earnest.

From an art historian's point of view, it was chaos from the beginning. Their sources were misleading, their deductions inaccurate (or so it is claimed) and the result was hybrid.

With a stableful of muses to call upon, they settled on another approach: they opened Pandora's box and all sorts of things jumped out – some good, some not so good.

Being an exhibition based on art for the lyric stage, we are spared the classic question: *"Prima la musica, doppo le parole"*, or the reverse, "First the words, then the music". We will concern ourselves with how various artists have given a sense of place and occasion to the antic activities that go on in front of scenery, in it, through it and out of it; or put more bluntly, how artists have risen (or fallen) to the challenge of opera.

The Renaissance held three settings as necessary for the theatre: a classic street for high drama, a less exalted street (with a banner indicating a house of pleasure) for comedy, and a forest for satyric (read bucolic) diversions. Add to those a noble interior, a rustic interior and a seashore and you have the locales for most of Baroque opera with the addition of a few clouds for ascents and descents of gods and demigods. A "hell's mouth" was also convenient.

The Operatic Muse is intended as a tribute to design, specifically that of operas of the past three hundred years that might be a part of an international opera-goer's experience. With a brief bow to the past, we will plunge into the repertory that has sustained opera houses for a considerable period. There are omissions not only of well-loved operas but of artists. Often the latter has led to the former as we have attempted to avoid the work, no matter how notable, of artists that have worked in the Southwest. This deprives us of the work of Conklin, Indiana, Isreal, Oenslager and Ter-Arutunian to name but a few. Our loss there may be compensated for by the inclusion of European artists whose names may be unfamiliar but whose work is vital to our concept of what is making the operatic world 'tick' today.

Operatic stage design has made a long and difficult journey through the years. From all-purpose house stock to the sumptuous extravaganzas linked in the public mind with 'grand' opera and with the names of directors, who often serve as their own designers, the road has been hazardous. Gone are the days of directors who arrived with a basket or so of costumes, a bag of rags which were to be the sets and the classic stage direction: "You go right, he'll go left".

Opera has come of age, dramatically as well as visually. Television as a medium has forced quality on opera; when treated as an art form and partner of the staged opera, it can give new meaning to the word "performance". Opera born with so many godparents has found additional ones. Designing for it still carries an awesome responsibility – that of fidelity to the spirit of the work itself.

For our purposes, in the beginning there was Gluck (*pace* Monteverdi, Cavalli, Piccinni, etc.). Certainly his 'reform' operas have proved the foundation for centuries of audiences and emotion on the stage cannot be carried further than Orfeo's lament, *"Che farò"*. St. Louis, in a worthy effort to emulate the fête books of the earliest operas, asked Louise Nevelson to create not only the décor for the opera but the design of the libretto itself. Mrs. Nevelson agreed and seven preliminary designs as well as the final libretto bear witness to her passion for the work which she celebrated in a poem made part of the book, *In Search of Orfeo.*

And now that Mozart's position in the world of opera has been secured, if not by transcendent quality then by Hollywood's "Oscars", it is easy to forget that the popularity of his operas underwent a series of eclipses (especially at the Metropolitan) which were forgiven with the emergence of certain singers whose personal magnetism caused the managements to dust off or reconstruct productions for them.

Now no self respecting opera house is without its versions of the *Da Ponte* trilogy (*Giovanni, Nozze* and *Così*); the opera seria are given consideration and *Zauberflöte* is cherished for all of its ambiguities and confusions – Masonic, political and otherwise.

Berman's *Giovanni* was to have been his last work for the stage and was the subject of a long and not unvitriolic *"Addio"* in the *Saturday Review.* It has certainly served the composer well and is refurbished as a monument of the 'old' Met. The maquette is a part of the complete suite of designs and plans which were preserved in an attempt not only to do homage to a great designer but give future scholars some concept of why the work held a position of unique respect for so long. Less respectful was Berman's covering of the proscenium of the *Piccola Scala* with his own inventions for *Così.* By dismantling his maquette for the production, the artist created the large architectural panel with its never-never land called "Naples".

Neither critics nor audiences have been particularly kind to Weber who is revived with *Freischütz* and rebuked for *Oberon* which seems unproducible even if you do have a soprano willing to sing "Ocean, thou mighty monster" while doing a backstroke across a lake. Less flamboyant is the moving scenery, attributed to the brothers Kautsky, for one of the transformation scenes as produced in Wiesbaden. The characters walk on a treadmill, the scenery passes in review and the opera stands still; or so it is reported.

Wagner presents an unending series of problems to the contemporary producer. The operas will probably never be freed from the Nazi embrace that was to befall them, not without reasonable cause. Taken on any level, the mystical *Parsifal* presents pitfalls, practical as well as philosophical.

Once the master was dead, the true believers as well as the sophisticated scoffers went to work. It could be argued that Wagner asked for it, but what has emerged in a hundred years surpasses sympathy. Appia was the first major artist to turn his attention to the monumental Wagnerian demands and in doing so transformed the way we look at any stage today. It was through light that he sought to illuminate the murkiness of Bayreuthian prosody as later Karajan sought the same ends by Stygian darkness.

For the purposes of this exercise, we will shift from the wildly imaginative early Hurry sketches for the Ring Cycle to his later renderings; from the first efforts at Bayreuth for *Parsifal* to Robert Wilson's contemporary dedication to the guileless fool.

If no self-respecting opera house is without its Mozart, no international company could exist without that colossus of Italian opera, Giuseppe Verdi. To the world, opera *is* Verdi and Verdi *is* opera. Four works from the later operas are included exhibiting extraordinarily differing approaches to the pieces. The complete suite of designs by Ming Cho Lee for *Il Trovatore* show the current dean of American stage designers in a typical mood. The small sketches are more usual; the larger renderings were done, by request, for exhibition purposes. Oliver Smith's ill-fated *Traviata* was an attempt to translate the 'fragile one's' story into grand opera house language. Created for the old Met, it was at its grandest in the second scene of the second act. (The first scene was seemingly conceived as a houseboat in a Louisiana swamp.) *Forza,* that vast panorama of love-fate-war-misery-religion spread over years and endless acts and scenes and characters and situations, was entrusted to Berman for its severely mutilated version that was mounted as a vehicle for Milanov's *"Pace, pace"* and the second act duet for tenor and baritone. Berman artfully moved the period of the opera from its original to his own Bermanesque period and produced several striking sets and a mass of hats. Glyndebourne chose Jean Pierre Ponnelle for its *Falstaff* and his costumes for Verdi's last hero are enchanting mementos of a memorable performance.

If Verdi towered over the nineteenth century with his dramatic masterpieces, Rossini answered back with his wise and witty comedies. (His late venture into the heavily dramatic *William Tell* was as disastrous as Verdi's early comedy, *Un Giorno di Regno.*) The cornerstone of comedy set to music is not all that comic being the first day of the *Beaumarchais-Figaro* trilogy. No one seems to mind the *Barber* being one of the longer operas in the repertoire; its seemingly unending waterfall of delicious melodies and extravagant showpieces delight decade after decade providing celebrated singers with well-oiled vehicles for bravura display. The motivating force is not so much the barber but the heroine whose vocal artillery can be called forth in full force whether she be mezzo-soprano or something higher. And in the naughty days of old she could interpolate her own choice of arias, songs or what you will for the lesson scene, sometimes accompanying herself. For its revival of the opera in the fifties, the Metropolitan turned to Berman with mixed results. Perhaps the most obvious visual pun was a pair of chairs for Dr. Bartolo and Don Basilio which perfectly reflected their physiognomy. Whether it was stage director Cyril Ritchard's concept or that of Berman, the second scene maquette demonstrates one of the most successful arrangements of four entrances at virtually center stage: a triumph of ingenuity.

The Italian preoccupation with volumes devoted to specific designers has preserved much of the works of such masters as Basoli, Quaglio, etc. Nothing came close to the elaborately bound and beautifully executed set of designs by Alessandro Sanquirico for La Scala in Milan. Each décor is more magnificent than the last and it is interesting to see Sanquirico's original design for *La Gazza Ladra,* an opera known more for its overture than frequency of performances.

Saint-Saëns' *Samson et Dalila,* an opera oratorio with two luscious arias for the mezzo siren, a touching scene for Samson at the millstone and a finale that brings down the house, is represented by the curious interpretation by Robert Edmond Jones of Grünewald's décor for the first scene of the third act. When Jones and Macgowan went to Europe to study 'Continental Stagecraft', Jones would criticize in visual terms, Macgowan in verbal. The collaboration was a turning point in stage design for the century as their adherents went on a light and form route while others chose a more decorative approach.

One hundred years after the triumphant opening of the

101. Ming Cho Lee, *Bomarzo,* Design for the Décor, "The Inner Spirit", ca. 1967.

Metropolitan Opera, the company could summon up its forces for but a brief excerpt from Gounod's *Faust* when it came time to celebrate its Gala. Once dubbed the *"Faust-spielhaus"*, the opera house has tried various approaches to its fallen old war horse and has found that hearts that once beat faster to the 'Soldiers' Chorus', wept over Marguerite's loss of chastity and were enthralled by the Devil himself with his promises of a Golden Calf, are not around now (or they don't carry their hearts on their sleeves or at least don't admit it enough to bring money from their pockets). The New York City Opera's version with evocative sets by Ming Cho Lee had a sense of time and place and a golden glow of time remembered.

Bizet's *Carmen* seems to have been thoroughly taken away from him. Once a mezzo's husband announced, "You must remember, this is my wife's opera." But *Carmen* also has 'belonged' to Roland Petit, Peter Brook, Frank Corsaro and Antonio Gaddes. The list is improbably long. Here we are content with four thumbnail sketches dating from Jo Mielziner's trip to Europe around 1920. They seem more the essence of *Carmen* than the grandiose efforts of others.

Jo Mielziner's career and that of Robert Edmond Jones were intertwined in many ways. Artistically, Mielziner inherited the latter's mantle. His design for *The Emperor Jones* for the Metropolitan Opera's excursion into American opera was a direct tribute to the older designer. The Louis Gruenberg opera itself was a vehicle for Lawrence Tibbett and was long considered one of the most effective American operas, a scarce commodity.

There exists an elite group of composers of Italian operas that the world could probably get by without: Giordano, Cilea and Zandonai occupy forgettable niches except for a few operas that cater to the whims of leading ladies who think of themselves in terms of glamour at any cost (the more the better). With a nod to this manifestation of the singer's caprice, Giordano's *Andrea Chénier* and its sumptuous Benois décor acknowledges (if not applauds) its existence.

Although there is a school of thought that would just as soon forget that Massenet existed, Manon returns in her poignant tale with some regularity. Despite shocking efforts to cut and rearrange her score, she lives best with all her limbs in place and one of the principal ones is the *"Cours la Reine"*. Benois's décor almost glitters as it reflects the cascades of her gavotte.

The Russian repertoire has presented ongoing problems for Western audiences. The early Diaghilev productions were sumptuous in the extreme and unleashed colour to Paris. Actually, the Metropolitan Opera used the cast-off Paris Opera production of *Boris* well into the third quarter of the century, sometimes with an Italian bass singing with a chorus going along in whatever language was found easiest. The current tendency is to use Russian, a language which had a curious outpouring some years ago in San Francisco when a Bulgarian bass, a Mexican mezzo, an English tenor, an Italian basso-buffo, a German bass and yet another one, this time Greek, made many un-united nations in the very hall of the signing of the UN Charter. The repertoire can be divided up into Tchaikovsky, Mussorgsky (either on the rocks or diluted by others), Rimsky-Korsakov and Prokofiev whose *War and Peace* has enough score in it to provide endless games of who will perform what. Stravinsky has been omitted as his is an international case.

Of the two Tchaikovsky operas that are twin pillars of the Russian repertoire, *Pique Dame* has never found quite the favor of *Onegin*. Its brilliance of score, its opportunity for spectacle, has often been overlooked in the public enthusiasm for Tatiana and her life and loves—or lack thereof. For his celebrated Sadler's Wells Theatre production, Leslie Hurry pulled out all the stops and was undoubtedly the ideal artist for the masterpiece. Two sets of drawings are included, the preliminary and the final designs, which give us an opportunity to watch a creative artist for the stage at work. Hurry's colours have often been called those of crushed jewels; here they are in their splendour.

Coq d'Or represents one of the great curiosities of the operatic stage. When performed as an opera-ballet, Diaghilev positioned the soloists between chorus members off stage while the dancers on stage represented the characters. Choosing a different approach from the original Diaghilev solution, various other producers have had the soloists perform their roles on stage. What has kept the opera alive is the magical musical material and the opportunity for lavish display. The Benois design for a Parisian production of 1927 gives one an idea of the splendour of the arrival of King Dodon in the first act. *Sadko,* as designed by Soudeikine, repeats the lavishness of approach but did not salvage the opera at its Metropolitan debut when it sank to the bottom of its own sea.

The mainstay of operatic repertoire, the always reliable Puccini, is represented by designs for the last scenes in his last opera, *Turandot.* One pair, the work of the ever dependable son of Alexandre Benois, is deliberately Oriental in feeling. The other, the work of the ever elusive grandson of Victor Emmanuel, Enrico d' Assia, is set in some surrealistic desert. Neither has much to do with Peking or Milan, which is where the opera probably takes place.

Der Corregidor, Hugo Wolf's only opera, has eluded a staged American production—probably with good reason. The interest in the suite of designs of Paolo Bregni lies not only in the fluency of his hand but his mastery of engraving. It is rare, if not unique, to have a suite of designs published as independent works of art.

Isolated out yonder in the never-never land of Allemagne, Debussy's only completed opera, *Pelléas et Mélisande,* holds a powerful attraction for many, a sense of unending ennui for others. The heroine presents the first of problems: she will not say where she comes from. And now that she is where she is, she is "not happy" here. Notable productions have dotted the scene for years, but Beni Montresor's mood sketches for Glyndebourne come very close to catching the ever elusive essence of the extraordinary work.

The Rake's Progress is finally achieving its just but long overdue place in the repertory. Stravinsky's parable had immense success in Glyndebourne in Hockney's homage-to-Hogarth sets and then at the Royal Opera Covent Garden in the production by Timothy O'Brien and Tazeena Firth. Combining an elegant sense of style, quicksilver changes and an immediacy of audience-stage empathy, the design team complemented Elijah Moshinsky's brilliant staging. The large maquette, being essentially the stage of the Royal Opera, proved a challenge to its designers and Air India as it was transported to America.

In Stravinsky's menagerie there are as many hybrid musical animals as the most extravagant of zoological parks. Arguably, there are three operas: *Mavra, Le Rossignol* and *The Rake's Progress.* Then there are ballets, ballet-operas, oratorio-operas and a host of ever satisfying experiments. *Le Renard* is undoubtedly sung, mimed and cries out for a scenic resolution of its staging. Mikhail Larionov was entrusted with the original décor and from his hand we have not only the scenery designs but costume sketches and drawings made during the rehearsals. (It is an interesting footnote to history that he repeated his designs on commission so there are several 'original' costume sketches for the "Fox Dressed as a Nun"—all quite original and quite the same.) On the other hand, *Le Rossignol* started as an opera before the First War, was picked up again and then converted into a ballet. Benois's monumental design is from its first incarnation. In this exhibition the Metropolitan's bow to Stravinsky is celebrated by Hockney's poster with its dedication.

Of the modern masters represented, Alban Berg is undoubtedly the most theatrical. Santa Fe, having been privileged to perform the American premiere of *Lulu,* has always had a unique stake in its fate in America. From the Metropolitan production, some years after Santa Fe's plunge, come Jocelyn Herbert's maquettes and costumes. With an unerring sense of the period, she has captured the suffocating decay of Berg's masterpiece.

Probably no other opera company has chosen Richard Strauss as one to share with Mozart the responsibility for the ever troublesome problem of holding up the repertory. But Santa Fe, blessed with a general director whose enthusiasm for the German master is equal to his command of the works themselves, has established a reputation for Strauss that is unequalled in this country. From the early excursions into *Ariadne* to the last operas it is a heritage of which to be proud. *Ariadne,* that improbable and ultimately unsuccessful attempt to graft an opera onto Molière's *Le Bourgeois Gentilhomme,* finds in Peter Rice a charming exponent of the decorative approach inherited from Ernst Stern. Nonetheless, the 'audience' remains a trifle fatigued by the plot which even poor Zerbinetta cannot fathom: a lady dying for love on a deserted island. Far from the mannered mock-tragedy of the eighteenth century is Robert O'Hearn's *Die Frau Ohne Schatten* which was designed for the first week of performances at the new Met. O'Hearn took seriously his task of bringing to the stage the last collaboration between Strauss and von Hofmannsthal using every device known to stage sorcery—a fabled opera house dealing with a fabled kingdom. The machinery took several years to work but the vision is certainly there, the mystery, the enchantment of a never-never (never) land. Barak's hut is seen with the bejeweled palace behind it. Transformation projections are revealed as integral parts of what was meant to be (and was) *'magnificence.'*

Possibly the most important American opera of the last quarter century, Roger Sessions' monumental *Montezuma* received its American premiere during the Bicentennial in Boston with the dean of American composers supervising what he came to call the "World Premiere". It was devised by Sarah Caldwell who also conducted; the choreography was by Amalia Hernandez and Delfina Vargas prepared the Aztec costumes which were executed under her supervision.

With *Dreigroschenoper* Kurt Weill blasted the twentieth century with one of its most insidious operas. (How many popular music fans would equate 'Satchmo' Armstrong's "Mack the Knife" with an operatic aria? Indeed, it is the "Moritat" which begins Weill's work.) Based on *The Beggar's Opera,* with a text by Brecht, there is certainly nothing quite like the work. Two artists are represented: William Pitkin for the original Theatre d' Lys production which set the work on its way as one of the great experiences in theatre in America, and Wolfgang Roth's quite scholarly and elegant renderings, each valid in their own way. A bit of superfluous blood is added with Berman's three sketches for the work as performed in Paris.

When one voices the claim that Gian Carlo Menotti's *Amahl and the Night Visitors* is the most successful opera ever written, one is besieged by angry

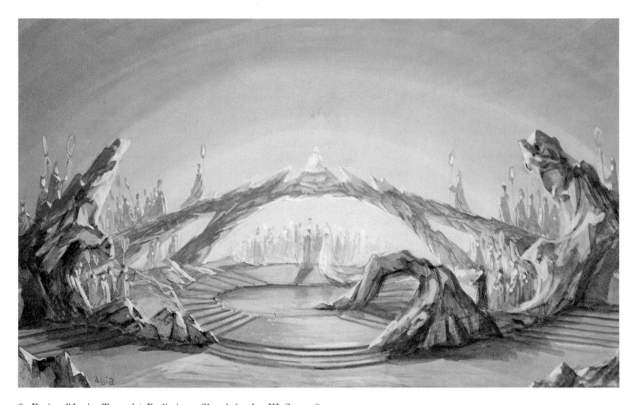

2. Enrico d'Assia, *Turandot,* Preliminary Sketch for Act III, Scene 2.

criticism. But *Amahl* was written for a specific purpose at a specific time for a particular appeal and audience. That it has transcended one television airing to be heard in 795 performances in a typical year attests that although tear-jerker it undoubtedly is, it is an effective one and very seldom fails to touch its audiences. It works. More cannot be said.

Although Berman's *Amahl* décor reflects a certain sense of fantasy (snow inside and outside the hovel), Beni Montresor's evocation of the realm of a mythical Maharaja in *Le Dernier Sauvage* is sheer magic as is the hunt with its three terrifying tigers romping playfully, surely one of the loveliest act-curtains ever devised.

The towering genius of British opera, Benjamin Britten, is represented by the décor by Kenneth Green for the original production of *Peter Grimes* at Sadler's Wells and the costume sketches of Tanya Moiseiwitsch for Ellen and Peter for the Metropolitan's production given during its first season in its new house. What was perhaps only a token gesture has become one of the mainstays of the repertory.

The brief nod to Hans Werner Henze with the inclusion of the small maquette for *The Young Lord* is no reflection on our admiration for his work. It is sentimental in that it was a debut performance, but playing by the rules laid down at the beginning, Henze's operas have been so much a part of the Santa Fe repertory that it is impossible to include many of them without their original American designers.

As the Allied troops marched north through Italy they rediscovered a strange and marvelous assemblage of monumental figures of carved stone virtually obliterated by thick undergrowth and tangled, forbidding vines. What was called the "Garden of the Monsters" was as mysterious to them as it was to later adventurers and as mysterious as the opera commissioned by the Washington Opera, performed there and later at the New York City Opera. *Bomarzo* now lies forgotten as once was the Orsini fantasy so beloved by Berman and Dali which inspired Alberto Ginastera's creation now represented by Ming Cho Lee's rendering of the grotto which keeps its haunting spirit remembered.

When the Metropolitan Opera unveiled its *Porgy* some fifty years after its premiere, it was interesting how little attention was paid to the fact that the original designer had been Sergei Soudeikine, whose vision of the prayer meeting, Act II, Scene 4, is included. (It is to be noted that the deluxe edition of the vocal score was signed by the composer, librettist and director but *not* the designer.)

In the vast flurry of 'white papers' which led to the formation of the 'Music Theatre' panel of the National Endowment for the Arts and subsequently the tongue twister, 'National Institute for Music Theatre', one question was asked: "Why is *Fidelio* more of an opera than *Carousel?*". Both are of serious nature (even lofty) with musical numbers tied together by either spoken dialogue or accompanied (accented) text. The answer was, of course, "One *is* as valid as the other". Using that as a point of departure the list of 'operas' that masquerade as 'musicals' could be quite impressive and arguing quite depressing. *Brigadoon* is certainly more fun that *Martha* (virtually anything is) but one is trotted out by 'opera' companies and the other is not (or almost never). *West Side Story* is a masterpiece on any terms. It is simply the company it keeps or perhaps the century it adorns.

The Operatic Muse has allowed us to traverse close to three hundred years of thinking about opera, what it means or rather what it was meant to mean and has come to be accepted as: an event with music and voice and dramatic content with sometimes more of one, sometimes more of another. Movement has usually played a part, usually of protagonists and antagonists in human form. Scenery itself has had its own choreography, especially in the Baroque period but also as late as the revival of *Thais* in California where two mobile motorways were is search of a resolution.

We have sought to illustrate a number of widely differing approaches. A few of them can be accepted as milestones against which all other productions can be measured: Benois's *Rossignol,* Berman's *Don Giovanni,* Hurry's Ring Cycle, Larionov's *Le Renard,* and Robert Wilson's *Parsifal.* Alexandre Benois, along with Leon Bakst, Mikhail Larionov and Natalia Gontcharova, so influenced Serge de Diaghilev that the explosion in Paris of Russian ballet with its introduction of Stravinsky and a host of collaborators has come to be known as probably the most brilliant outpouring of creative talent in the history of not only dance but also music and design. Eugene Berman's early training in St. Petersburg as an architect brought a creative eye to the problems of music, dance and drama and their interrelationship; and Berman, not accidently, was a close friend of Stravinsky. Leslie Hurry was persuaded from his career as a distinguished painter into stage design by Robert Helpmann and his last work, *Mazeppa,* was to have been his American debut for the Boston Opera. It is a long leap to Wilson, born in Texas, nurtured as the most creative talent in current theatrical design, being idolized in Europe and now being recognized in the Southwest. Each has sought to conquer on his own terms. When Mrs. Nevelson made her debut as a designer she felt that same need to conquer, the 'Operatic Muse' masquerading (perhaps) as Orpheus:
Orfeo—
Oh, Orfeo, the glorious,
I have finally caught up with you:
Divine image—eternal presence.

Robert L. B. Tobin

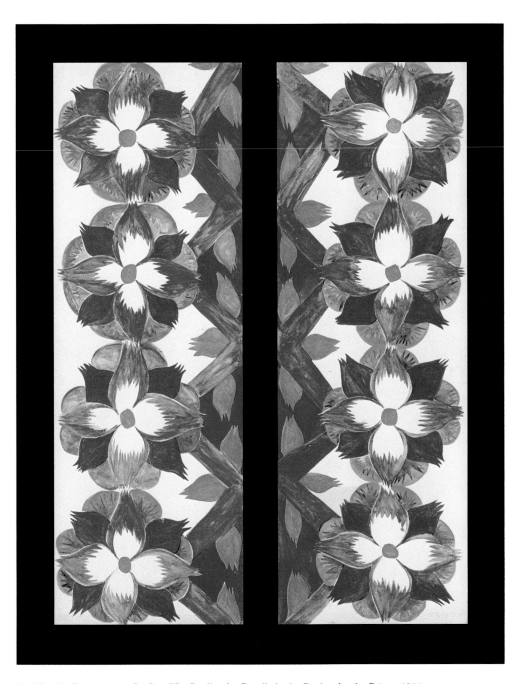

56. Natalia Gontcharova, *Le Coq d'Or,* Studies for Details in the Design for the Décor, 1914.

9. John Lee Beatty, *Carousel,* Design for the Décor, Act II, Scene 6, "Graduation", ca. 1978.

CATALOG OF THE EXHIBITION

ENRICO D'ASSIA
1927–date of death unknown, Italian

Turandot, an unfinished opera in 3 acts by Giacomo Puccini; libretto by Renato Simoni and Giuseppe Adami after Carlo Gozzi; probably for *La Scala,* Milan.

   1. Preliminary Sketch for Act III, Scene 1, date unknown. Watercolor and gouache on paper, 6½ × 11″.
Signed at lower left: *'Assia'.*

   2. Preliminary Sketch for Act III, Scene 2, date unknown.
Watercolor and gouache on paper, 6⅜ × 11″.
Signed at lower left: *'Assia'.*
Illustrated on page 12.

LÉON BAKST
1866–1924, Russian

Boris Godounov, an opera in 3 acts, book and music by Mussorgsky, décor and costumes for Act II by Bakst, other designs by Constantin Juon and Ivan Bilibine; presented by the *Ballets Russes* in a mixed program of ballet and opera at the *Théâtre de Champs-Élysées,* Paris, 1913.

   3. Costume Design for Marina, 1913. Watercolor, gold paint and pencil on paper, 10½ × 8¼″.
Signed and inscribed at lower right: *'Boris Godounov, Marina, Bakst'.*

JOHN LEE BEATTY
1948–   , American

Carousel, a musical by Richard Rodgers, book and lyrics by Oscar Hammerstein; for an unrealized production, ca. 1978. All of these designs are pencil, watercolor and gouache on illustration board and all measure 20 × 30″ (sheet size).

   4. Design for the Décor, Act I, Scene 1, "Amusement Park".
Initialled and inscribed at lower right: *'Amusement Park "Carousel" Act one scene 1 JLB'.*

   5. Design for the Décor, Act I, Scene 2, "A Path in the Woods".
Initialled and inscribed at lower right: *'A Path in the Woods "Carousel" Act One Scene 2 JLB'.*

   6. Design for the Décor, Act I, Scene 3, "Nettie's Spa".
Initialled and inscribed at lower right: *'Nettie's Spa "Carousel" Act One Scene 3 JLB'.*

   7. Design for the Décor, Act II, Scene 3, "Up There".
Inscribed at lower right: *'Up There "Carousel" Act Two, Scene 3'.*

   8. Design for the Décor, Act II, Scene 5, "The Cottage".
Inscribed at lower right: *'The Cottage "Carousel" Act Two—Scene 5'.*

   9. Design for the Décor, Act II, Scene 6, "Graduation".
Initialled and inscribed at lower right: *'Graduation "Carousel" Scene 6 JLB'.*
Illustrated on page 16.

ALEXANDRE BENOIS
1888–1960, Russian

Le Rossignol, music by Igor Stravinsky; choreography by Romanov; costumes and décor by Benois; first performed by Diaghilev's *Ballets Russes* at the Paris Opera on May 26, 1914.

   10. Design for the Décor, Act III, "The Throne Room", 1914. Gouache on paper laid down on canvas, 39 × 43″.
Signed and dated at lower left: *'Alexandre Benois 1914'.*
Illustrated on page 18.

Le Coq d'Or, an opera in 3 acts with prologue and epilogue by Rimsky-Korsakov; libretto by Vladimir Ivanovich Belsky after Pushkin; for the 1927 Paris Opera production.

   11. Design for the Décor, Act III, 1926. Pencil on paper, 18½ × 24¾″.
Signed and dated at lower left: *'A. Benois 1926'.*
Inscribed at lower center: *'Le Coq d'Or Acte III'.*

Manon, an opera in 5 acts by Massenet; book by Henri Meilhac and Philippe Gille based on Prevost's *L'Historie du Chevalier des Grieux et de Manon Lescaut;* for the 1931 production at the *Teatro Colón,* Buenos Aires.

10. Alexandre Benois, *Le Rossignol,* Design for the Décor, Act III, "The Throne Room", 1914.

12. Design for the Décor, Act III, Scene 2, "Open-Air Theatre", 1931. Ink, watercolor and gouache on paper, 14½ × 22½".
Signed at lower left: *'Alexandre Benois'*.
Inscribed at bottom: *'Manon Acte III. 2^{me}Effet. 1931 Théâtre Colon Buenos Aires'*.

Andrea Chénier, an opera by Tommaso Giordano; libretto by Illica; for the 1951 production at *La Scala,* Milan.

13. Design for the Décor, Act I, Scene 3, 1949. Watercolor, pencil, ink and gouache on paper, 12¾ × 19¾".
Signed and inscribed at bottom: *'Alexandre Benois Andrea Chénier 3 I 49'*.

NICOLA BENOIS
1901– , Russian, currently living in Switzerland

Turandot, an unfinished opera in 3 acts by Giacomo Puccini; libretto by Simoni and Adami after Gozzi; for the 1959 production at *La Scala,* Milan. All of these designs measure 9⅜ × 13¼".

14. Design for the Décor, 1958. Watercolor, colored pencil and ink on paper.
Signed and dated at lower right: *'Nicola Benois 1958'*.

15. Design for the Décor, Act II, Scene 2, 1958. Colored pencil and ink on paper.

16. Design for the Décor, Act III, Scene 1, 1958. Watercolor, colored pencil and ink on paper.
Signed and dated at lower right: *'Nicola Benois 58'*.

Parsifal, an opera in 3 acts by Richard Wagner; production unknown.

17. Design for the Décor, Act III, Scene 1, 1960. Gouache, watercolor, pastel and crayon on paper, 19 × 25".
Signed and dated at lower right: *'Nicola Benois, 60'*.
Inscribed at lower left: *'Parsifal III atto 1 scena'*.

EUGENE BERMAN
1899–1972, American, born in Russia

L'Opera de Quat'Sous, (The Threepenny Opera or *The Beggar's Opera),* a musical in a prologue and 3 acts by Kurt Weill; libretto by Bertolt Brecht after John Gay's "The Beggar's Opera"; for a 1937 Paris production.

18. Design for the Décor, Prologue, 1937. Ink and watercolor on paper, 8 × 12½" (sight).
Initialled and inscribed at top: *'L'Opera de 4 Sous Prologue E. B. 1937'*.

19. Design for the Décor, "Studies of Faces", 1937. Ink and watercolor on paper, 7½ × 10½".
Initialled and dated at lower left: *'EB 1937'*.
Inscribed at top: *'L'Opera de 4 Sous'*.

20. Design for the Décor, 1937. Ink, watercolor and gouache on paper, 7 × 10⅛".

Amahl and the Night Visitors, the first opera written for television with music and libretto by Gian Carlo Menotti; produced by NBC on December 24, 1951 and staged at Indiana University on February 21, 1952.

21. Design for the Décor, maquette, 1952. Mixed media, 17 × 31 × 18".

22. Design for the Décor, 1952. Ink and watercolor on paper mounted on board, 7¾ × 10¾".
Initialled and dated at lower center: *'E.B. 1952'*.
Inscribed at top and bottom: *'Amahl and the Night Visitors To Tommy (Amahl) Shippers* (top) *with very sincere appreciation and friendship* (bottom)'.

La Forza del Destino, an opera in 4 acts by Giuseppe Verdi; libretto by Francesco Maria Piave, based on the play, *"Don Alvaro o la fuerza del sino",* by Angel Saavedra, Duke of Rivas, and on a scene from the play, *"Wallensteins Lager"* by Friedrich Schiller; produced at the Metropolitan Opera House, New York, in 1952.

23. Design for the Décor, Act I, Scene 1, maquette, 1952. Mixed media, 10¼ × 16⅝ × 8⅝".
Initialled and dated on front 2 panels: *'E.B. 1952'*.

24. Design for the Décor, Act I, Scene 2, maquette, 1952. Mixed media, 10½ × 17⅛ × 10½".
Initialled on third panel from front: *'E.B. 1952'*.
Inscribed on fourth panel from front: *'La Forza del Destino 1952'*.

25. Design for the Décor, Act II, maquette, 1952. Mixed media, 10⅝ × 17 × 10½".
Initialled at top of back panel: *'E.B. 1952'*.

26. Design for the Décor, Act III, Scene 2, 1952. Ink and gouache on paper, 5⅞ × 9⅜".
Initialled in lower center: *'E.B.'*.
Inscribed at lower left and right: *'La Forza del Destino Act III'*.

Il Barbiere di Siviglia, an opera buffa in 2 acts by Rossini with libretto by Cesare Sterbini; for the 1954 production at the Metropolitan Opera House, New York.

27. Costume Design for Don Basilio, 1954. Ink, watercolor and gouache on paper, 11¾ × 8⅞".
Initialled and dated at lower center: *'E.B. 1954'*.
Inscribed at upper right with *'Il Barbiere di Siviglia'* and at lower left with *'Don Basilio'*.

40. Eugene Berman, *Don Giovanni,* Design for the Décor, Act I, Scene 2, "Blue Sky and Castle", maquette, 1957.

28. Costume Design for Doctor Bartolo, Act II, 1953.
Ink and gouache on paper, 11¾ × 8⅞".
Initialled and dated at upper center: 'E.B. 1953'.
Inscribed at upper center above artist's initials
with 'Il Barbiere di Siviglia' and at lower left with
'Doctor Bartolo'.

29. Design for the Décor, Act II, "Two Chairs for
Doctor Bartolo and Don Basilio", 1953.
Watercolor, ink and pastel on paper,
13⅝ × 10¾".
Initialled and dated at lower center: 'E.B. 1953'.
Inscribed at lower left and right: 'Doctor Bartolo'
and 'Don Basilio' and at lower center '2 chairs for
Bartolo & Don Basilio'.

30. Design for the Décor, Act II, maquette, 1953.
Mixed media, 9½ × 15¼ × 6⅞".
Initialled and dated on second panel: 'E.B. 1953'.

Così fan Tutte, an opera in 2 acts by Wolfgang
Amadeus Mozart; libretto by Lorenzo da Ponte; for
the 1955 production at the *Piccola Scala*, Milan.

31. Design for the Décor, maquette, mounted flat,
1955. Mixed media, 32¼ × 22¼".
Initialled and dated at center: 'E.B. 1955'.
Inscribed at center: 'Così fan tutte Piccola Scala
Milano'.

Don Giovanni, an opera by Wolfgang Amadeus
Mozart; staged by Herbert Graf for the 1958
production at the Metropolitan Opera House, New
York.

32. Design for the Presentation Plate, 1957.
Watercolor and ink on paper, 10⅜ × 7¾".
Initialled and dated at lower center: 'E.B. 1957'.

33. Two Designs for the Décor, 1957, Watercolor and
ink on paper, each 5⅞ × 8⅞".

34. Costume Design for Don Giovanni, 1957.
Watercolor and ink on paper, 10⅜ × 7¾".
Initialled and dated at lower center: 'E.B. 1957'.

35. Costume Design for Donna Elvira, Act I, Scene 2,
1957. Watercolor, gouache and ink on paper,
9¾ × 6⅞".
Initialled and dated at lower center: 'E.B. 1957'.

36. Costume Design for Elvira, 1957. Watercolor,
gouache and ink on paper, 8¾ × 5⅞".
Initialled and dated at lower center: 'E.B. 1957'.

37. Costume Design, 1957. Watercolor, gouache and
ink on paper, 10⅛ × 6¾".
Initialled and dated at lower center: 'E.B. 1957'.

38. Costume Design for Courtesan, 1957. Watercolor,
gouache and ink on paper, 9⅞ × 6½".
Initialled and dated at lower center: 'E.B. 1957'.

39. Costume Design for *Il Commendatore*, 1957.
Watercolor and ink on paper, 9¾ × 6⅞".
Initialled and dated at lower center: 'E.B. 1957'.

40. Design for the Décor, Act I, Scene 2 "Blue Sky
and Castle", maquette, 1957. Mixed media,
13 × 27 × 17⅝".
Inscribed with title, artist's initials and date on
verso: 'Don Giovanni, Act I, Scene 2 Blue Sky &
Castle E.B. 1957'.
Illustrated on page 20.

Otello, an opera in 4 acts by Giuseppe Verdi; libretto
by Arrigo Boito after Shakespeare; for the 1963
production at the Metropolitan Opera House, New
York.

41. Design for Backdrop, Act III, "Lion of St. Mark",
1963. Ink, gouache and watercolor on illustration
board, 8¾ × 11⅞".
Initialled, dated and inscribed at bottom: 'Otello
Act III E.B. 1963 Banner of St. Marc (Curtain)'.

42. Design for the Décor, Act IV, "Bed and Front",
1963. Ink, watercolor and gouache on paper,
14¾ × 10¾".
Initialled, dated and inscribed at upper center:
'Otello Act IV Bed and Front E.B. 1963'.

MAURICE BLOND
Birthdate unknown-   , French

L'Opéra de Quat'Sous, (The Threepenny Opera), a
musical in 3 acts by Kurt Weill; libretto by Bertolt
Brecht; for a 1972 Paris production. All of these
designs are pencil, crayon and watercolor on paper,
mounted on board, and all measure 17 × 12".

43. Costume Design for the *Chef de Police, 1972.*.
Signed and dated at lower right: 'M. Blond '72'.
Inscribed on mount at bottom: 'L'Opéra de
quat'Sous. Chef de Police'.

44. Costume Design for *Polly, Fiancée de Chef de
Police, 1972.*
Signed and dated at lower right: *72 M. Blond.*
Inscribed on mount at bottom: 'L'Opéra de
quat'sous Polly fiancée de Mac, Chef de Voleurs'.

45. Costume Design for the *Chanteur de
Complimentes, 1972.*
Signed and dated at lower right: 'M. Blond 72'.
Inscribed on mount at bottom: 'L'Opéra de
quat'sous Le Chanteur de complimentes'.

46. Costume Design for *Mac, Chef des Voleurs, 1972.*
Signed and dated at lower right: 'M. Blond 72'.
Inscribed on mount at bottom: 'L'Opéra de
Quat'Sous Mac, chef des voleurs'.

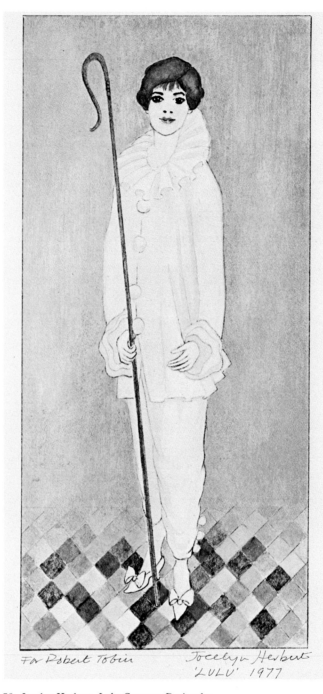

For Robert Tobin   Jocelyn Herbert
                     'LULU' 1977

58. Jocelyn Herbert, *Lulu,* Costume Design for
    Harlequin, Act II, 1977.

47. Costume Design for the *Mendiant, 1972.*
Signed and dated at lower left: *'M. Blond 72'.*
Inscribed on mount at bottom: *'L'Opéra de
quat'sous Le mendiant, faux infirme'.*

PAOLO BREGNI
1937– , Italian

Der Corregidor, a comic opera in 4 acts by Hugo Wolf;
for a production at the *Teatro Regio, Torino,* in 1978.
All of these designs are engravings and all measure
19¾ × 27⅜″ (sheet size), 1978.

48. Design for the Décor.
Numbered, title and signed at bottom: *'21/30 "Der
Corregidor" di Hugo Wolf Bregni 1978'.*

49. Design for the Décor.
Numbered and signed at bottom: *'21/30 Bregni
1978'.*

50. Design for the Décor.
Numbered and signed at bottom: *'21/30 Bregni
1978'.*

51. Design for the Décor.
Numbered and signed at bottom: *'21/30 Bregni
1978'.*

MSTISLAV DOUBOUJINSKY
1875–1957, Russian

Boris Godounov, an opera in 3 acts, book and music by
Mussorgsky; for the 1953 production of the
Metropolitan Opera, New York.

52. Design for the Décor, "The Throne Room", 1952.
Gouache on paper mounted on board, 8 × 11⅛″.
Initialled at lower right: *'MD'*
Signed on mount: *'M. Douboujinsky'.*

NATALIA GONTCHAROVA
1882–1962, Russian

Le Coq d'Or, an opera-ballet in 3 acts with music by
Nikolai Rimsky-Korsakov and libretto by Vladimir
Belsky based on a fairy tale by Alexander Pushkin and
adapted by Alexandre Benois. Produced by Serge de
Diaghilev for the *Ballets Russes* at the *Théâtre
National de l'Opéra* in Paris in 1914 with choreography
by Michel Fokine. This opera-ballet represents
Gontcharova's first collaboration with Diaghilev.

53. Design for the Décor, Act I, 1913–14. Watercolor
and pencil on paper, 12¼ × 16″.
Signed and inscribed at lower left:
'N. Gontcharova "Coq d'Or" '.

54. Design for the Décor, 1913–14. Watercolor and
pencil on paper, 14¾ × 21″.
Signed at upper right: *'N. Gontcharova'.*

55. Studies for Details in the Design for the Décor,
1914. Gouache on illustration board, 2 panels each
measuring 21 × 7⅜″.
Cover illustration.

56. Studies for Details in the Design for the Décor,
1914. Gouache on illustration board, 2 panels each
measuring 21 × 7¼″.
Signed at lower right of right panel:
'N. Gontcharova'.
Illustrated on page 15.

KENNETH GREEN
Birthdate unknown– , English

Peter Grimes, an opera in by 3 acts by Benjamin
Britten; libretto by Montagu Slater derived from
George Crabbe's poem, "The Borough"; produced at
Sadler's Wells Theatre, London, in 1945.

57. Design for the Décor, Act I, Scene 2, "The Boar"
Interior, 1945.
Ink and watercolor on paper, 8½ × 15″.
Signed and dated at lower right: *'Kenneth Green
1945'.*
Inscribed at bottom: *' "Peter Grimes"—Benjamin
Britten. Sadler's Wells 1945 Act I, Sc 2. "The
Boar" interior'.*

JOCELYN HERBERT
1917– , English

Lulu, an opera in 3 acts (the third act unfinished) with
music and libretto by Alban Berg derived from Frank
Wedekind's *Erdgeist* and *Die Büchse der Pandora;* for
the 1977 production at the Metropolitan Opera House,
New York.

58. Costume Design for Harlequin, Act II, 1977. Color
lithograph, 19¾ × 13¾″ (sheet size).
Signed and dated at lower right: *'Jocelyn Herbert
'LULU' 1977'.*
Inscribed at lower left: *'For Robert Tobin'.*
Illustrated on page 22.

The following costume designs are ink and watercolor
on paper mounted on board and each measures
17 × 12″. All of these designs have identifying labels
at the right and many include the artist's notations
concerning fabrics at right.

59. Costume Designs for Schigolch and Dr. Schön, 1977.

60. Costume Designs for Lulu and Alwa, 1977.

61. Costume Designs for Lulu and Geschwitz, 1977.

62. Four Costume Designs for Dr. Schön, 1977.

63. Four Costume Designs for Lulu, 1977.

64. Four Costume Designs for Lulu, 1977.

80. Leslie Hurry, *Siegfried,* Design for the Décor, Act II, 1954–55.

65. Four Costume Designs for Lulu, 1977.

66. Design for the Décor, maquette, 1977. Mixed media, 24$\frac{1}{2}$ × 37 × 31$\frac{3}{4}$".

67. Design for the Décor, maquette, 1977. Mixed media, 24$\frac{1}{2}$ × 37 × 31$\frac{5}{8}$".

68. Design for the Décor, maquette, 1977. Mixed media, 24$\frac{1}{2}$ × 36$\frac{3}{4}$ × 31$\frac{5}{8}$".

DAVID HOCKNEY
1937–   , English

69. Stravinsky Poster for the Metropolitan Opera, 1981. Color serigraph, 80 × 35".
Signed and dedicated at bottom: 'For Robert Tobin David Hockney'.

LESLIE HURRY
1909–1978, English

Der Ring des Nibelungen, an operatic tetralogy with music and libretto by Richard Wagner; for the 1954 Royal Opera Covent Garden production.

Ten Preliminary Designs for the Décor, 1954; all are ink, watercolor, felt-tip pen and crayon on paper.

70. *Das Rheingold,* 7$\frac{1}{2}$ × 11$\frac{1}{8}$".
Signed and dated at lower right: 'Leslie Hurry/54'.

71. *Das Rheingold,* Act I, 7$\frac{1}{2}$ × 11$\frac{1}{8}$".
Signed and dated at lower right: 'Leslie Hurry/54'.
Inscribed at lower left: 'Rheingold, Act I'.

72. *Das Rheingold,* Act I, Scene 3, 7$\frac{5}{8}$ × 11$\frac{1}{8}$".
Signed and dated at lower right: 'Leslie Hurry/54'.
Inscribed at lower left: 'Rheingold, Act I, Sc III'.

73. *Die Walküre,* Act I, 7$\frac{7}{8}$ × 12$\frac{3}{4}$".
Signed and dated at lower right: 'Leslie Hurry/54'.
Inscribed at lower left: 'Walküre, Act I'.

74. *Die Walküre,* Act II, 7$\frac{7}{8}$ × 12$\frac{7}{8}$".
Signed and dated at lower right: 'Leslie Hurry/54'.
Inscribed in left margin and at lower left: 'Walküre, Act II'.

75. *Die Walküre,* Act III, 8 × 12$\frac{3}{4}$".
Signed and dated at lower right: 'Leslie Hurry/54'.
Inscribed at lower left: 'Walküre, Act III'.

76. *Siegfried,* Act I, 8 × 12$\frac{3}{4}$".
Signed and dated at lower right: 'Leslie Hurry/54'.
Inscribed at lower left: 'Siegfried Act I'.

77. *Siegfried,* Act II, 8 × 12$\frac{3}{4}$".
Signed and dated at lower right: 'Leslie Hurry/54'.
Inscribed at lower left: 'Siegfried Act II'.

78. *Götterdämmerung,* Act II, 8 × 12$\frac{3}{4}$".
Signed and dated at lower right: 'Leslie Hurry/54'.
Inscribed at lower left: 'Götterdämmerung Act II'.

79. *Götterdämmerung,* Sketch, 8 × 10$\frac{3}{4}$".
Signed at lower right: 'Leslie Hurry'.
Inscribed in lower margin: 'Götterdämmerung Covent Garden Opera Final Sc/ Rough Preliminary'.

80. *Siegfried,* Design for the Décor, Act II, 1954–55. Ink and watercolor on paper, 17$\frac{3}{8}$ × 23".
Signed and dated at lower right: 'Leslie Hurry/55'.
Inscribed at bottom: 'Siegfried Act II'.
Illustrated on page 24.

Pique Dame, an opera in 3 acts with music and libretto by Tchaikovsky after Pushkin; for the 1965 Sadler's Wells Theatre production in London.

81. Seven Preliminary Designs for the Décor, 1965. Ink, watercolor, felt-tip pen and crayon on paper, top design measures 7$\frac{1}{4}$ × 10$\frac{1}{2}$", six lower designs measure 8$\frac{3}{4}$ × 10$\frac{3}{4}$".
Each signed at bottom: 'Leslie Hurry'.
Top design inscribed with 'Queen of Spades'.

82. Three Final Designs for the Décor, Act I, Scenes 1 and 2, 1965. Ink, watercolor, felt-tip pen and crayon on paper, each 11$\frac{1}{4}$ × 15$\frac{1}{8}$".

83. Three Final Designs for the Décor, Act II, Scenes 1 and 2, 1965. Ink, watercolor, felt-tip pen and crayon on paper, each 11$\frac{3}{8}$ × 15$\frac{1}{8}$".
Each signed at lower right: 'Leslie Hurry'.

84. Four Final Designs for the Décor, Acts I, II, III, 1965. Ink, watercolor, felt-tip pen and crayon on paper, each 11$\frac{1}{4}$ × 15$\frac{1}{8}$".
Two lower designs signed at bottom: 'Leslie Hurry'.

Mazeppa, an opera in 3 acts with music and libretto by Tchaikovsky and Viktor Burenin. At the time of his death, Hurry was working on the designs for the production for the Boston Opera; this project was abandoned. These designs are ink and colored pencil on paper and all measure 12 × 17" (sight); ca. 1978.

85. Design for the Décor, Act I, Scene 1.
Inscribed at top: 'Act I Sc I Mazeppa'.

86. Design for the Décor, Act I, Scene 2.
Inscribed at top: 'Act I Sc II Mazeppa'.

87. Design for the Décor, Act II, Scene 1.
Inscribed at top: 'Act II Sc I Mazeppa'.

88. Design for the Décor, Act II, Scene 2.
Inscribed at top: 'Act II Sc 2 Mazeppa'.

ROBERT EDMOND JONES
1887–1954, American

The following renderings of European stage productions were completed by Jones in 1922 during a

94. Mikhail Larionov, *Le Reñard,* Design for the Décor, ca. 1922.

trip he and Kenneth Macgowan took to study design trends on the Continental stage. These renderings were included as plates in their subsequent book, *Continental Stagecraft,* published in 1922.

Das Rheingold, first part of the operatic tetralogy by Richard Wagner; designed by Adolf Linnebach and Leo Pasetti for the National Theatre of Munich.

89. "Alberich's Cave", Gouache and ink on paper, 8 × 11″ (image size).
Illustrated on page 28.

Samson et Dalila, an opera in 3 acts by Camille Saint-Saëns, book by Ferdinand Lemaire; designed by Isaac Grünewald for the Royal Opera in Stockholm.

90. "The Mill", Act III, Scene 1, Gouache, watercolor and ink on paper, 7¾ × 9″ (image size).
Illustrated on page 29.

KAUTSKY BROTHERS, Attributed to
Dates unknown, German

Oberon, an opera in 3 acts with music by Weber; libretto by Planché after Wieland's poem based on the story *"Huon de Bordeaux"* in *La Bibliothèque Bleue;* for a Wiesbaden Opera House production.

91. Design for Moving Diorama (also used for *Armide*), ca. 1900. Watercolor and gouache on graph paper, 11 × 34¼″.
Inscribed at right.

ANONYMOUS, German
ca. 1890

Samson et Dalila, an opera by Camille Saint-Saëns; for a Wiesbaden Opera House production.

92. Design for the Décor, Act III, 'Showing the City Standing and the City Fallen'. Watercolor, gouache and ink on graph paper, 12¼ × 17″.
Inscribed at top.

These two unsigned renderings for the Wiesbaden Opera House illustrate two techniques for changeable scenery used around the turn of the century.

PAUL KNAUERHASE
1858–1942, German

Tannhäuser, an opera in 3 acts with music and libretto by Richard Wagner. Knauerhase worked primarily at the *Hoftheater* (Court Theatre) in Hannover from 1884–1926 where he was appointed Royal Court Theatrical Painter.

93. Design for the Décor, early 20th century. Watercolor and pencil on paper mounted on board, 12½ × 17¼″.

MIKHAIL LARIONOV
1881–1964, Russian

Le Renard, a ballet burlesque with voices in one act by Igor Stravinsky based on a Russian folk tale adapted by Charles Ferdinand Ramuz; produced by Serge de Diaghilev, with choreography by Bronislava Nijinska, for the *Ballets Russes* at the *Théâtre National de l'Opéra,* Paris, in 1922.

94. Design for the Décor, ca. 1922. Watercolor on paper, 15 × 21¾″.
Initialled at lower right: *'M.L.'.*
Illustrated on page 26.

95. Costume Design for The Cock, 1921. Watercolor, gouache and pencil on paper, 20½ × 13½″.
Inscribed and signed at upper left and right: *'Renard M. Larionov Coq'.*
Initialled and dated at lower left: *'M 921'.*

96. Costume Designs for The Fox, Cock and Nun, 1920. Pencil on paper, 12¾ × 19″.
Signed at lower right: *'M. Larionov 920'.*

97. Sketch of Nun and Fox, ca. 1922. Ink on paper, 11 × 8¾″.
Inscribed and initialled at lower right: *' "Renard" M.L.'*

98. "The Nun and Cock in Conversation", 1921. Pencil on paper, 12¾ × 19½″.
Signed and dated at lower left: *'M. Larionov 1921'.*

99. "The Nun and Cock in Conversation", 1920. Pencil on paper, 11½ × 18½″.
Signed and dated at lower left: *'M. Larionov 1920'.*

100. "The Nun and Cock in Conversation", 1920. Pencil on paper, 11½ × 18½″.
Signed and dated at lower left: *'M. Larionov 920'.*

MING CHO LEE
1930– , American, born in Shanghai

Bomarzo, an opera in 2 acts by Alberto Ginastera; for the Opera Society of Washington, Washington, D.C., 1967.

101. Design for the Décor, "The Inner Spirit", ca. 1967. Gouache and pencil on paper, 5⅛ × 9⅜″.
Initialled at lower right: *'MCL'.*
Illustrated on page 8.

Faust, an opera in 4 acts by Charles François Gounod; book by Jules Barbier and Michel Carré; for the New York City Opera production in 1968.
The following designs are pencil and watercolor on yellow lined paper and all measure 3¼ × 5½″.

102. Three Designs for the Décor, ca. 1968.

89. Robert Edmond Jones, *Das Rheingold,* "Alberich's Cave", 1922.

90. Robert Edmond Jones, *Samson et Dalila,* Act III, Scene 1, "The Mill", 1922.

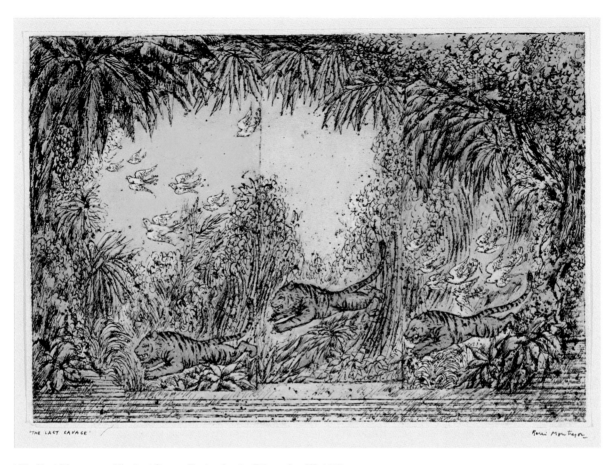

120. Beni Montresor, *The Last Savage,* Design for the Décor, Act III, 1963.

103. Two Designs for the Décor, ca. 1968.

104. Two Designs for the Décor, ca. 1968.

105. Two Designs for the Décor, ca. 1968. Pencil, watercolor and colored marker on yellow lined paper, 3½ × 6″.

Il Trovatore, an opera in 4 acts by Giuseppe Verdi; book by Salvatore Cammarano; for the 1980 San Diego Opera production. The following designs are pencil and watercolor on paper and measure 4 × 6″, ca. 1980.

106. Three Designs for the Décor.

107. Three Designs for the Décor.

108. Three Designs for the Décor.

109. Design for the Décor, 10 × 6½″.

110. Design for the Décor, 15½ × 24″.

111. Design for the Décor, 15½ × 24″.

112. Design for the Décor, 15½ × 24″.

113. Design for the Décor, 15½ × 24″.

JO MIELZINER
1901–1976, American

Carmen, an opera in 4 acts by Georges Bizet; book by Ludovic Halevy.

114. Three Small Scenic Sketches, ca. 1921. Gouache and watercolor on paper, 1¼ × 2″ each.

The Emperor Jones, an opera in 2 acts by Louis T. Gruenberg based on a play by Eugene O'Neill; for the 1932 production of the Metropolitan Opera, New York.

115. Design for the Décor, "The Throne Room", 1931. Ink, watercolor and pencil on paper, 11 × 18″. Illustrated on page 4.

TANYA MOISEIWITSCH
1914–   , English

Peter Grimes, an opera in 3 acts by Benjamin Britten; libretto by Montagu Slater derived from George Crabbe's poem, "The Borough", for the 1966 production of the Metropolitan Opera, New York.

116. Costume Design for Peter Grimes, 1965. Gouache on illustration board, 18 × 12″.
Signed and dated at lower left: *'T. Moiseiwitsch 1965'.*
Inscribed at upper left and right: *'Grimes Peter Grimes'.*

117. Costume Design for Ellen Orford, 1965. Gouache on illustration board, 18 × 12″.
Signed and dated at lower left: *'T. Moiseiwitsch 1965'.*

Inscribed at upper left and right: *'Ellen Orford Peter Grimes'.*

BENI MONTRESOR
1926–   , Italian

Pelléas et Mélisande, an opera in 5 acts by Claude Debussy; libretto from Maurice Maeterlinck's play of the same name; for the 1962 Glyndebourne Opera production. Both of these designs are ink and watercolor on paper mounted on board.

118. Mood Sketch, Act I, 1962. 10⅛ × 14⅜″.
Signed and dated at lower left: *'Beni Montresor 1962'.*
Inscribed and signed on mount: *'Pelléas et Mélisande Beni Montresor'.*

119. Mood Sketch, Act I, 1962. 6⅜ × 9″.
Inscribed and signed on mount: *'Pelléas et Mélisande Beni Montresor'.*

The Last Savage, an opera by Gian Carlo Menotti; for the 1964 Metropolitan Opera production, New York. Both of these designs are ink and watercolor on paper mounted on board.

120. Design for the Décor, Act III, 1963. 11⅜ × 16¾″.
Inscribed and signed on mount: *'The Last Savage Beni Montresor'.*
Illustrated on page 30.

121. Design for the Décor, Act III, Scene 2, 1963. 11⅜ × 16⅝″.
Inscribed and signed on mount: *'The Last Savage Beni Montresor'.*

LOUISE NEVELSON
1900–   , American, born in Russia

Orfeo and Euridice, an opera in 1 act by Christoph Willibald Gluck; libretto by Raniero de Calzabigi; for the 1984 production at the Opera Theater of St. Louis. All of these designs were completed in that same year and all are gouache, acrylic paint and permanent marker on parchment paper.

122. Working Design for the Libretto. 21 × 15½″.
Inscribed in left margin: *'Orfeo p. 22'.*

123. Working Design for the Libretto. 21 × 15½″.
Inscribed in bottom margin: *'Orfeo p. 27'.*

124. Working Design for the Libretto. 21 × 15½″.
Inscribed in bottom margin: *'Orfeo p. 30'.*

125. Working Design for the Libretto. 21 × 15½″.
Inscribed in bottom margin: *'Orfeo p. 33'.*

126. Working Design for the Libretto. 15½ × 21″.
Inscribed in bottom margin: *'Orfeo (2 page spread) p40 p41'.*

138. Robert O'Hearn, *Die Frau Ohne Schatten,* Design for the Décor, "Cave Temple", 1966.

127. Working Design for the Libretto. 21 × 15¹/₂ ".
Inscribed in bottom margin: *'Orfeo p. 44'.*

128. Working Design for the Libretto. 20³/₄ × 15¹/₂ ".
Inscribed in bottom margin: *'Orfeo p. 46'.*

TIMOTHY O'BRIEN
1929–   , English
TAZEENA FIRTH
1935–   , English

The Rake's Progress, an opera in 3 acts and epilogue by
Igor Stravinsky; libretto by W. H. Auden and Chester
Kallman; for the 1978–79 production of the Royal
Opera Covent Garden.

129. Design for the Décor, Act I, maquette, ca. 1978.
Mixed media, 27¹/₂ × 29¹/₂ × 38 ".

The following designs are ink on paper and all
measure 9 × 7 "(sight), ca. 1978.

130. Costume Design.

131. Costume Design for The Shadow, Act I, Scene 1.
Inscribed at lower right and upper right: *'Act I Sc
1'* and *'9'.*

132. Costume Design for Tom Rakewell.
Inscribed at bottom and upper right: *'Tom
Rakewell'* and *'4'.*

133. Costume Design for Rakewell, Act II, Scene 1.
Inscribed at lower left and at right: *'Act 2 Sc. 1
Rakewell'*, *'2'* and *'begins Act 2, Sc. 1 in bedraggled
undress'.*

134. Costume Design for Baba the Turk.
Inscribed at lower left and upper right: *'Baba the
Turk'* and *'11'.*

135. Costume Design for Baba the Turk, Act II, Scene
3.
Inscribed at bottom and upper right: *'Act 2 Sc 3
Baba the Turk'* and *'12'.*

136. Costume Design, Act III, Scene 1.
Inscribed at upper right and center: *'225'* and *'Act
3 Sc 1 A B C × 2 Kennington Ladies out
Shopping for the Home'* (with names of ladies
listed).

137. Costume Design for Anne Truelove, Act III,
Scene 3.
Inscribed at lower left and upper right: *'Act 3 Sc 3
Anne Truelove'* and *'7'.*

ROBERT O'HEARN
1921–   , American

Die Frau Ohne Schatten, an opera in 3 acts by Richard
Strauss; libretto by Hugo von Hofmannsthal; for the
1966 production of the Metropolitan Opera, New York.

138. Design for the Décor, "Cave Temple", 1966. Ink,
watercolor, silver and gold paint on paper,
8¹/₂ × 13¹/₂ " (sight).
Illustrated on page 32.

139. Design for the Décor, "Underground River", 1966.
Ink, watercolor, gold paint and glitter on paper,
8¹/₂ × 13 " (sight).

140. Design for the Décor, "Dyer's House", Scrim,
1966. Batik, 28 × 38³/₄ ".
Inscribed at bottom: *' 'Die Frau' Dyer's House
Scrim—1–2¹/₂ "=1'0"'.*

141. Design for the Décor, Finale Drop, 1966. Batik,
29¹/₂ × 38 ".
Inscribed at bottom: *' "Die Frau" Finale Drop.
Trans. plus apron (continue design) ¹/₂ "=1'0"'.*

142. Design for the Décor, Act I, Scene 2, maquette,
1966. Mixed media, 24 × 41 × 35 ".
This model was commissioned by the New York
Public Library for an exhibition that was mounted
to coincide with the opening of the new
Metropolitan Opera House in 1966.

WILLIAM PITKIN
1925–   , American

The Threepenny Opera, a musical drama in a prologue
and 3 acts by Kurt Weill; libretto by Bertolt Brecht
after John Gay's "The Beggar's Opera"; for the 1954
production at the Theatre d'Lys, New York.

143. Design for the Décor, "Newgate Prison", 1954.
Pencil, ink and gouache on board, 19³/₄ × 29³/₄ ".
Signed at lower right: *'William Pitkin'.*
Inscribed at lower left: *'The Threepenny Opera
Newgate Prison'.*

144. Design for the Décor, "Original Stable", 1954.
Pencil, ink and watercolor on paper, 11 × 18 "
(sight).

145. Design for the Décor, "The Street" (Prologue),
1954. Pencil, ink and watercolor on paper,
15 × 28 " (sight).
Signed, dated and inscribed at bottom; *' "The
Threepenny Opera" The Street William Pitkin
'54'.*

146. Design for the Décor, "The Bordello in Wapping",
1954. Ink and watercolor on paper, 16 × 26 "
(sight).
Signed and inscribed at bottom: *' "The
Threepenny Opera"– The Bordello in Wapping–
William Pitkin '54'.*

147. Design for the Décor, "The Street", 1954. Ink and
watercolor on paper, 17 × 21¹/₂ ".
Signed and inscribed at bottom: *' "The
Threepenny Opera" Street William Pitkin'.*

164. Alessandro Sanquirico, *La Gazza Ladra,* Design for the Décor, "Woman Before the Tribunal", 1817.

148. Design for the Décor, "The Street as an Arcade",
1954. (This design was not used.) Gouache,
watercolor and ink on brown paper, 14½ × 20½ ".
Signed and inscribed at bottom: *'The Street as an
Arcade   The Threepenny Opera   Wild Wings on
sides   William Pitkin '54'.*

149. Design for the Décor, Act II, Scene 1, "The
Stable", 1954. (This design was not used.)
Gouache, watercolor and ink on paper,
8½ × 14½ ".
Signed and inscribed at bottom: *'The Threepenny
Opera   Stable   Act II Sc. 1   William Pitkin '54'.*

150. Design for the Décor, Portal Door Masking, Stage
Left, 1954. Ink and watercolor on illustration
board, 19¾ × 11 ".
Inscribed in right margin: *'5 Stage Left Masking'.*

151. Design for the Décor, Portal Door Masking, Stage
Right, 1954. Ink and watercolor on illustration
board, 19¾ × 11½ ".
Inscribed in right margin: *'1 Stage Rt.
Masking   The Threepenny Opera   Designed by
William Pitkin'.*

152. Design for the Décor, Adjustable Masking, Stage
Left, 1954. Ink and watercolor on illustration
board, 19¾ × 14¾ ".
Signed and inscribed at bottom: *'Threepenny
Opera St. Left Adj. Wing   William Pitkin'.*

153. Design for the Décor, Adjustable Masking, Stage
Right, 1954. Ink and watercolor on illustration
board, 19¾ × 14¾ ".
Signed and inscribed at bottom: *'Threepenny
Opera St. Right Adj. Wing   William Pitkin'.*

154. Design for the Décor, Backwall Drop, 1954.
Pencil, ink and gouache on illustration board,
19¾ × 29¾ ".
Signed and inscribed at lower right: *'The
Threepenny Opera   Backwall Drop   William
Pitkin'.*

155. Design for the Décor, maquette, 1954. Mixed
media, 8¾ × 20⅛ × 3¾ ".
Inscribed at left: *' "The Threepenny Opera"   Weill
& Brecht...Designed By William Pitkin   Theatre
d'Lys NYC   1954'.*

HELEN POND
1924–   , American
HERBERT SENN
1924–   , American

The Young Lord, an opera in 3 acts by Hans Werner
Henze; libretto by Ingeborg Bachmann based on a tale
by Wilhelm Hauff; for the New York City Opera's 1973
production.

156. Design for the Décor, maquette, 1979. Mixed
media, made from the original pieces of the 1973
model, 8⅝ × 12⅞ × 5¼ ".
Inscribed at bottom: *'Mr. Robert Tobin as Sir
Edgar in Hans Werner Henze's "The Young Lord".
New York State Theatre. 1973'.*

JEAN PIERRE PONNELLE
1932–   , French

Falstaff, a comedic opera in 3 acts by Giuseppe Verdi;
libretto by Boito after Shakespeare; for the 1976
Glyndebourne Festival production.

157. Costume Design for Sir John Falstaff, 1976. Pencil
heightened with white gouache on brown paper,
21 × 14½ " (sight).
Initialled and inscribed at lower right: *'Sir John
Falstaff N: I JP '76'.*

158. Costume Design for *Sir John Falstaff,* 1976.
Pencil heightened with white and gray gouache on
brown paper, 20½ × 14½ " (sight).
Initialled and dated at lower right: *'JP 76'.*
Inscribed at upper right: *'Sir John Falstaff N:II'.*

PETER RICE
1928-   , English, born in India

Ariadne auf Naxos, an opera in one act by Richard
Strauss; libretto by Hugo von Hofmannsthal for the
Royal Opera Covent Garden, 1968.

159. Design for the Décor, Act II, 1968. Ink and
watercolor on paper, 14 × 18½ ".
Signed and inscribed at bottom: *'Act II "Ariadne"
Peter Rice '68'.*

WOLFGANG ROTH
1910–   , American

L'Historie du Soldat, an opera by Igor Stravinsky;
libretto by Charles Ferdinand Ramuz; for the 1935–36
production at the Corso Theater, Zurich.

160. Design for the Décor, 1935–36. Mixed media on
paper, 22 × 30 ".
Signed and inscribed at lower right: *'Corso
Theater, Zurich 1935–36   Wolfgang Roth'.*

The Threepenny Opera, a musical drama in prologue
and 3 acts by Kurt Weill; libretto by Bertolt Brecht
after John Gay's "The Beggar's Opera"; for the 1965
production at the New York City Center.

161. Design for the Décor, Prelude, 1965. Ink and
watercolor on paper, 14 × 20 ".
Signed and dated at lower right: *'W. Roth '65'.*
Inscribed at lower left and at upper center:
'Prelude'.

168. Sergei Soudeikine, *Sadko,* Design for the Décor, "The Novgorod Coast", ca. 1930.

162. Design for the Décor, 1965. Ink and watercolor on paper, 14 × 20″.
Signed and inscribed at bottom: 'City Center—N.Y. W. Roth '65' and inscribed at upper center: 'Die 3 Groschen—Oper 1965'.

163. Design for the Décor, 1973–74. Ink on paper, 14 × 20″.
Signed and dated at lower right: 'Roth 73–74'.
Inscribed at lower center: 'Die 3 Groschen—Oper Munchen'.
This design was for a later production in Munich.

ALESSANDRO SANQUIRICO
1777–1849, Italian

La Gazza Ladra, an opera by Rossini, libretto by Gherardini; for the 1817 production at *La Scala,* Milan. Sanquirico was the the chief designer for *La Scala* from 1806–1833. His nostalgic neoclassicism became the perfect foil for the new operas of Bellini, Rossini, Donizetti and Piccinni.

164. Design for the Décor, "Woman Before the Tribunal", 1817. Ink on paper, 11¼ × 14⅜″ (image).
Signed at lower right: 'Alessandro Sanquirico'.
Illustrated on page 34.

OLIVER SMITH
1918–   , American

La Traviata, an opera in 4 acts by Giuseppe Verdi; libretto by F.M. Piave; adapted from *La Dame aux Camélias,* Alexandre Dumas' controversial novel of the well-known Parisian courtesan Alphonsine Plessis; for the 1958 production of the Metropolitan Opera, New York.

165. Design for the Décor, Act I, 1958. Pencil, ink and watercolor on paper, 19 × 23″.
Signed at lower right: 'Oliver Smith'.
Inscribed at lower left: 'Act I   Traviata Met. Opera Prod.'.

166. Design for the Décor, Act III, 1958, Pencil, ink and watercolor on paper, 18½ × 23″.
Signed at lower right: 'Oliver Smith'.
Inscribed at lower left: 'Act III Traviata Met. Opera Prod.'.

Martha, an opera in 4 acts by Flotow; libretto by Friedrich Wilhelm Riese after Saint-Georges' ballet-pantomime, *Lady Henriette ou La Servante de Greenwich;* for the 1960 production of the Metropolitan Opera, New York.

167. Design for the Décor, Act I, Scene 1, 1960. Ink and watercolor on paper, 17 × 25″.
Signed and dated at lower right: 'Oliver Smith—'60'.
Inscribed at lower left: 'Martha Sc. 1.1.'.

SERGEI SOUDEIKINE
1882–1946, Russian

Sadko, an opera with book and music by Rimsky-Korsakoff; for the 1930 production of the Metropolitan Opera, New York.

168. Design for the Décor, "The Novgorod Coast", ca. 1930. Gouache on illustration board, 20½ × 38¾″.
Signed at lower left: 'Soudeikine'.
Illustrated on page 36.

Porgy and Bess, a musical by George Gershwin; lyrics by DuBose Heyward; first performed by the Theater Guild in Boston at the Colonial Theater on September 30, 1935.

169. Design for the Décor, Act II, Scene 4, ca. 1935. Oil on canvas, 16 × 28″.
Signed at lower left: 'Soudeikine'.

DELFINA VARGAS
Birthdate unknown–   , American

Montezuma, An opera in 3 acts by Roger Sessions; libretto by Giuseppe Antonio Borgese; for the Opera Company of Boston production in 1976. These three designs are colored pencil and felt-tip marker on illustration board and all measure 22 × 16″. They are labelled with the artist's name at lower center.

170. Costume Design, ca. 1976.

171. Costume Design, ca. 1976.

172. Costume Design. ca. 1976.

JOSÉ VARONA
1930–   , American

Bomarzo, an opera in 2 acts by Alberto Ginastera; for the 1967 production of The Washington Opera Society, Washington, D. C.; sets by Ming Cho Lee and costumes by José Varona.

173. Costume Design for Abul, 1967. Pencil, gouache and watercolor on paper, 21 × 15″.
Signed and dated at lower right: 'J. Varona NY. 67'.
Inscribed at lower left: ' "Bomarzo" Washington Opera S. #12 Abul'.

174. Costume Design for Francesco Orsini, 1967. Pencil, gouache and watercolor on paper, 20 × 14⅞″.
Signed and dated at lower right: 'J. Varona NY. 67'.
Inscribed at lower left: ' "Bomarzo" #10 Pier Francesco Orsini'.

178. Robert Wilson, *Parsifal,* Design for the Décor, End of Prologue, 1985.

Faust, an operatic tragedy in 4 acts by Charles François Gounod; libretto by Jules Barbier and Michel Carre; for the New York City Opera's 1968 production.

175. Costume Designs for Old Faust and the Old Scholar, 1968. Pencil and watercolor on illustration board, 20 × 15″.
Signed and dated at lower right: *'J. Varona N Y. 68'.*
Inscribed at lower left: ' *"Faust" (New York City Opera)'* and at upper center: *'Old Faust #1, Old Scholar #167'.*

176. Costume Designs for Faust and Mephisto, 1968. Pencil and watercolor on illustration board, 20 × 15″.
Signed and dated at lower right: *'J. Varona N Y. 68'.*
Inscribed at lower left: ' *"Faust" (New York City Opera)',* and at upper center: *'Mephisto # 126 Faust # 125'.*

177. Panel of Six Costume Designs, 1968. Pencil and watercolor on illustration board, 14¾ × 19⅞″.
Signed at lower right: *'J. Varona N Y. 68'.*
Inscribed at lower left: ' *"Faust" (New York City Opera)',* and in upper margin: *'Poor Woman #195 Poor Woman #196   Clerk #190   Old Burgar #170   Poor Woman #197   Poor Woman #198'.*

ROBERT WILSON
1941–   , American

Parsifal, an opera by Richard Wagner; for an unrealized production, 1985. These designs are graphite on paper.

178. Design for the Décor, End of Prologue. 32⅛ × 40¼″.
Signed and inscribed at lower right: *'Prologue "Parsifal" R. Wilson '85'.*
Illustrated on page 38.

179. Design for the Décor, Act I. 26 × 40½″.
Signed and inscribed at lower right: *'Act I "Parsifal" R. Wilson '85'.*

180. Design for the Décor, Act II. 26⅛ × 40″.
Signed and inscribed at lower right: ' *"Parsifal" Act Two   R. Wilson '85'.*

181. Design for the Décor, Act II, 26⅛ × 40″.
Signed and inscribed at lower right: ' *"Parsifal" Act II   R. Wilson '85'.*

182. Design for the Décor, End of Act II. 27½ × 39⅜″.
Signed and inscribed at lower right: ' *"Parsifal" Act II   End R. Wilson '85'.*

183. Design for the Décor, Act III. 26⅛ × 40⅛″.
Signed and inscribed at lower right: ' *"Parsifal" Act III   R. Wilson '85'.*

SELECTED BIBLIOGRAPHY

Aronson, Arnold. *American Set Design,* New York: Theatre Communications Group, 1985.

Arundell, Dennis. *The Story of Sadler's Wells: 1683–1964.* New York: Theatre Arts Books, 1965.

Blum, Daniel. *Opera World, Seasons 1952–53, 1953–54.* New York: G. P. Putnam's Sons, 1955.

Bowlt, John E. *Russian Stage Design: Scenic Innovation, 1900–1930 — from the Collection of Mr. and Mrs. Nikita D. Lobanov-Rostovsky.* Jackson, Mississippi: Mississippi Museum of Art, 1982.

Crowell's Handbook of World Opera, compiled by Frank Ledlie Moore. New York: Thomas Y. Crowell Company, 1961.

The Encyclopedia of Opera, Leslie Orrey, ed. New York: Charles Scribner's Sons, 1976.

Gatti, Carlo. *Il Teatro alla Scala: Nella Storia e Nell' Arte (1778–1963).* Milan: Ricordi, 1964.

Kochno, Boris. *Diaghilev and the Ballets Russes.* New York: Harper and Row, 1970.

Pecktal, Lynn. *Designing and Painting for the Theatre.* New York: Holt, Rinehart and Winston, 1975.

Who's Who in Opera, Maria F. Rich, ed. New York: Arno Press, 1976.

Who's Who in the Theatre: A Biographical Record of the Contemporary Stage, 16th Edition. Ian Herbert, ed. London: Pitman Publishing Ltd., 1977.

Design, typesetting and printing by
Best Printing Company, Austin, Texas
Photography by Michael Smith